Serving From the Heart

FOR YOUTH

Finding Your Gifts and Talents for Service

PARTICIPANT WORKBOOK

CHURCH OF THE
RESURRECTION
RESOURCES

Abingdon Press

Nashville

07 08 09 10 11 12 13 14 15 16—10 9 8 7 6 5 4 3 2 1

Cover Design: Kelly Chinn

Contents

Hit Your S.T.R.I.D.E.

You're about to embark on a journey. You may be wondering, "Why am I here? Where is this going to lead?" The fact that you've made it to this point is evidence that the Holy Spirit is already at work in your life. This workbook will serve as your guide as you seek to discover certain truths:

❖ You are uniquely created by God.
❖ God has given you significant gifts.
❖ God has a plan and purpose for your life.
❖ As a Christian, you are called to serve.

To take it a step further, you will examine how this knowledge affects the church as a whole. God also has a specific design and purpose for the church—the Body of Christ.

> "I know the plans I have for you," says the LORD, . . . "plans . . . to give you a future and a hope." (Jeremiah 29:11, NLT)

Let's begin our trek. This book emerged out of the collective experience of the Spiritual Gifts Discovery Team at The United Methodist Church of the Resurrection (COR), in Leawood, Kansas. The Spiritual Gifts Discovery Team is a group of men and women dedicated to helping others discover how God has designed them with the gifts that make it possible for them to be in service within the body of Christ. As we have taught Spiritual Gifts Discovery over the years, we have heard many stories of how people in our church and in others have struggled with the concept of serving God. We have heard people say:

❖ I'm not qualified to serve God.
❖ I couldn't possibly have an impact.
❖ Serving God is a duty; it's not something that should be enjoyed. After all, didn't Christ say, "Deny [yourself], take up [your] cross and follow me"?
❖ There are so many people that I'm not going to be missed.
❖ That's the pastor's job.

❖ I've had a bad experience in the past, and I'm not going to do that again.

We grieve when we hear statements like this, because we do not believe that this is the way God wants us to think or feel. God's plan for the church calls for each of us to be unique—with different gifts, talents, resources, styles, dreams, and experiences—so that together, as the unified body of Christ, we can accomplish God's work in this world. That may sound overwhelming to some of us. If you're feeling intimidated by that notion, imagine how the disciples must have felt when Jesus commanded them to "go . . . and make disciples of all nations."

The Great Commission

> Jesus came and said to them, "All authority in heaven and on earth has been given to me. Go therefore and make disciples of all nations, baptizing them in the name of the Father and of the Son and of the Holy Spirit, and teaching them to obey everything that I have commanded you. And remember, I am with you always, to the end of the age." (Matthew 28:18-20)

The disciples were a rather ragtag bunch of fellows—mostly uneducated, and certainly not the most reliable or confident group. Just a few weeks earlier, they had run for their lives when Jesus was arrested. They had to have been full of self-doubt and feeling overwhelmed about what he was commanding them to do. They had forgotten that Jesus had promised to send them a counselor, comforter, teacher, and helper—the Holy Spirit (see Acts 1:4-5).

The Holy Spirit did arrive as promised (at Pentecost—see Acts 2:1-20). The Holy Spirit empowered and equipped the disciples to build the Christian church. This was by intentional design. It was God's plan for the way the church should function today. The Bible is our ultimate guidebook for helping us to discover God's will for our individual lives and as members of the body of Christ.

At The Church of the Resurrection, we have used a metaphor to help us understand the greatest adventure we will ever experience—the Christian life. This metaphor is called *Spiritual Summits,* and it compares the Christian life to hiking in the mountains.

The term *Spiritual Summits* is a metaphor for our faith journey. Like mountain climbers, we all begin down in the valley (in the world). When we decide to hike a mountain, we choose from a variety of paths the one best suited to our level of hiking experience. There is a path that suits every level of hiker. Beginning hikers travel best on gently sloped, paved trails. Steep ascents challenge experienced climbers who want to scale cliffs. Likewise, when we walk with Christ, different paths and trails fit our level of spiritual experience.

At Church of the Resurrection, we have identified three levels to describe the different maturity levels of a faith journey: Seeker, Explorer, and Guide. Likewise, there are four major types of trails, each one with various levels of paths for us to take: Worship, Grow, Give, and Serve.

At every level, we *Worship* God. As we seek to grow our faith, we choose from different paths along the *Grow* trail to find one that is a good match for our maturity level. On the *Give* trail, for example, we may move from irregular, small offerings to a regular commitment to giving, to tithing, in the Guide level.

Spiritual Gifts
Talents
Resources
Individuality
Dreams
Experiences

In this book, we will look at the *Serve* trail. On the *serve* trail, many different paths are available. The answer to which one is right for you depends on your unique S.T.R.I.D.E. as you hike the *Spiritual Summits*.

S.T.R.I.D.E.

No two persons are exactly alike. We have different abilities, dreams, and preferences—among other things. S.T.R.I.D.E. is an acronym that we use to describe the way Christians are unique as we hike the *Spiritual Summits*. Just as we each choose different paths, we also have unique strides as we make our journey. One person walks slowly, the next walks quickly, and another skips all the way. As Christians, we are expected to use our spiritual gifts to serve others and to glorify God. God has created each of us with a specific purpose in mind, giving us varied Spiritual gifts, Talents, Resources, Individual styles, and Dreams, and incorporating our Experiences in ways that are designed to help us extend the "great invitation" and fulfill the Great Commission. In this book, we will examine these six elements of our unique God-design and seek to understand God's plan for the church as well as God's purpose for our lives.

Now that we've discussed the "what" and the "why" of our journey, it's time to head out on the trail. Our first and foundational step will be to explore the subject of spiritual gifts, the "S" of our S.T.R.I.D.E. And speaking of foundations, the authoritative foundation for spiritual gifts is God's Word—the Bible.

Chapter 1: The Bible and Spiritual Gifts

"For we are God's masterpiece. He has created us anew in Christ Jesus, so that we can do the good things he planned for us long ago."

(Ephesians 2:10, NLT)

Do you ever wonder why you're here; how you fit in to the big picture; what you—a teenager—can do to serve God? The truth is that many of us ask ourselves these questions from time to time, no matter how old we are. We're not sure if God has a plan for our lives or that we even have any skills that God can use. The good news is this: God does have a plan for each of our lives and has given each of us the skills and abilities we need to see that plan come to life. These abilities are called *spiritual gifts*.

Our first hint about spiritual gifts in the New Testament comes when Jesus' earthly ministry is coming to a close, and he begins to prepare his disciples to carry on his mission without him. Think about it for a second: There stands this group of mostly uneducated, unsophisticated, uncommitted men; and Jesus is telling them that not only is he going to leave them, but he also expects them to continue his work when he's gone. No wonder they were confused and frightened! Then Jesus gives them a promise: He will not leave them alone in this mission.

> [12]*"I tell you the truth, anyone who believes in me will do the same works I have done, and even greater works, because I am going to be with the Father. . . .* [15]*If you love me, obey my commandments.* [16]*And I will ask the Father, and he will give you another Advocate, who will never leave you.* [17]*He is the Holy Spirit."* (John 14:12, 15-17a)

After Jesus' resurrection, he reminded them of this promise:

> [4]*He commanded them, "Do not leave Jerusalem until the Father sends you the gift he promised, as I told you before.* [5]*John baptized with water, but in just a few days you will be baptized with the Holy Spirit. . . .* [8]*You will receive power when the Holy Spirit comes upon you. And you will be my witnesses, telling people about me everywhere."* (Acts 1:4b-5, 8a, NLT)

And that is exactly what happened. The Holy Spirit came upon the disciples and those who were gathered with them shortly after Jesus' ascension, and the disciples immediately began preaching the gospel. In one day, 3000 people joined the church.

However, this power the disciples received didn't make them perfect. They still had faults and failings; but through the power of the Holy Spirit, they were able to accomplish what they weren't able to before. God was able to use them in spite of their faults. In fact, that was part of God's plan.

Like the disciples, we are simply "earthen vessels." The cracks and imperfections are holes that allow God's light to shine through. The Holy Spirit working through us—not our own strengths or abilities—is what makes our gifts powerful. That takes some of the pressure off us, doesn't it?

Spiritual gifts are the foundation to understand God's plan for how we can best serve God, the church, and people in the community. Discovering our gifts enables us to be most effective in service. It also helps us find a place of service that we'll get excited about. We never really look forward to doing something on a regular basis if we're not very good at it.

> Through the power of the Holy Spirit, they were able to accomplish what they weren't able to before.

For example, Justine loves skating. She goes to the skating rink several times a week and is a great skater. Her brother, Mark, on the other hand, loves baseball. Sometimes he invites her to play baseball with him and his friends if he needs an extra player. Baseball isn't Justine's thing. She can't throw or hit the ball; but, at least, she can catch it if someone throws it to her. She leaves those pickup games feeling demoralized, a failure—not at all like when she leaves the skating rink, feeling confident and capable.

The same principle holds true when we try to figure out how we should serve God or what God's plans for us entail. We tend to enjoy doing what we do well. A special ability in a particular area may be a clue about what our spiritual gifts are. This doesn't mean that we won't need some training or practice. But through our God-given spiritual gifts, we have the capacity, the underlying abilities necessary for success.

The Bible has quite a bit to say about spiritual gifts, but some of us have never even heard the term *spiritual gifts*. Let's spend a little time exploring Scripture to better understand what the gifts are, who has them, and what their purpose is.

1 Corinthians 12:1, 4-7

> [1]*And now, dear brothers and sisters, regarding your question about the special abilities the Spirit gives us. I don't want you to misunderstand this....*

[4]There are different kinds of spiritual gifts, but the same Spirit is the source of them all. [5]There are different kinds of service, but we serve the same Lord. [6]God works in different ways, but it is the same God who does the work in all of us. [7]A spiritual gift is given to each of us so we can help each other.

According to verse 1, what are spiritual gifts? Who receives spiritual gifts?

According to verses 1 and 4, who is the source of the gifts?

Verses 4-6 contain an interesting compare/contrast section. What do you think it means?

According to verse 7, what is the purpose of spiritual gifts?

1 Corinthians 12:8-11

[8]To one person the Spirit gives the ability to give wise advice; to another the same Spirit gives a message of special knowledge. [9]The same Spirit gives great faith to another, and to someone else the one Spirit gives the gift of healing. [10]He gives one person the power to perform miracles, and another the ability to prophesy. He gives someone else the ability to discern whether a message is from the Spirit of God or from another spirit. Still another person is given the ability to speak in unknown languages, while another is given the ability to interpret what is being said. [11]It is the one and only Holy Spirit who distributes all these gifts. He alone decides which gift each person should have.

What are the spiritual gifts listed in this passage? (Don't worry if you don't understand them all. They'll be defined later.)

Based on the verses we've looked at so far, do you think that anyone receives *all* of the gifts? Why, or why not? What does that mean for us?

According to verse 11, who decides which gift(s) we do receive? Why is that important?

1 Corinthians 12:12-22, 27-31

[12]*The human body has many parts, but the many parts make up one whole body. So it is with the body of Christ.* [13]*Some of us are Jews, some are Gentiles, some are slaves, and some are free. But we have all been baptized into one body by one Spirit, and we all share the same Spirit.*

[14]*Yes, the body has many different parts, not just one part.* [15]*If the foot says, "I am not a part of the body because I am not a hand," that does not make it any less a part of the body.* [16]*And if the ear says, "I am not part of the body because I am not an eye," would that make it any less a part of the body?* [17]*If the whole body were an eye, how would you hear? Or if your whole body were an ear, how would you smell anything?*

[18]*But our bodies have many parts, and God has put each part just where he wants it.* [19]*How strange a body would be if it had only one part!* [20]*Yes, there are many parts, but only one body.* [21]*The eye can never say to the hand, "I don't need you." The head can't say to the feet, "I don't need you."*

[22]*In fact, some parts of the body that seem weakest and least important are actually the most necessary. . . .*

[27]*All of you together are Christ's body, and each of you is a part of it.* [28]*Here are some of the parts God has appointed for the church:*

> *first are apostles,*
> *second are prophets,*
> *third are teachers,*
> *then those who do miracles,*
> *those who have the gift of healing,*
> *those who can help others,*
> *those who have the gift of leadership,*
> *those who speak in unknown languages.*

[29]*Are we all apostles? Are we all prophets? Are we all teachers? Do we all have the power to do miracles?* [30]*Do we all have the gift of healing? Do we all have the ability to speak in unknown languages? Do we all have the ability to interpret unknown languages? Of course not!* [31]*So you should earnestly desire the most helpful gifts.* (NLT)

The apostle Paul compares the church to the human body in the above passage. This is where we get the term *the body of Christ*. What point do you think Paul was trying to make with this analogy?

Based on your understanding of verses 29-31, do you think that there are any spiritual gifts that every Christian receives? Why is that important?

What gifts are listed in verses 29-31?

Romans 12:4-8

> [4]*Just as our bodies have many parts and each part has a special function,* [5]*so it is with Christ's body. We are many parts of one body, and we all belong to each other.*
>
> [6]*In his grace, God has given us different gifts for doing certain things well. So if God has given you the ability to prophesy, speak out with as much faith as God has given you.* [7]*If your gift is serving others, serve them well. If you are a teacher, teach well.* [8]*If your gift is to encourage others, be encouraging. If it is giving, give generously. If God has given you leadership ability, take the responsibility seriously. And if you have a gift for showing kindness to others, do it gladly.* (NLT)

According to verse 6, spiritual gifts have been given to whom?

What is the message in verse 6?

What gifts do you find listed in verses 6-8?

Ephesians 4:1-7, 11-16

[1]As a prisoner for the Lord, then, I urge you to live a life worthy of the calling you have received. [2]Be completely humble and gentle; be patient, bearing with one another in love. [3]Make every effort to keep the unity of the Spirit through the bond of peace. [4]There is one body and one Spirit—just as you were called to one hope when you were called—[5]one Lord, one faith, one baptism; [6]one God and Father of all, who is over all and through all and in all.

[7]But to each one of us grace has been given as Christ apportioned it. . . .

[11]It was he who gave some to be apostles, some to be prophets, some to be evangelists, and some to be pastors and teachers, [12]to prepare God's people for works of service, so that the body of Christ may be built up [13]until we all reach unity in the faith and in the knowledge of the Son of God and become mature, attaining to the whole measure of the fullness of Christ.

[14]Then we will no longer be infants, tossed back and forth by the waves, and blown here and there by every wind of teaching and by the cunning and craftiness of men in their deceitful scheming. [15]Instead, speaking the truth in love, we will in all things grow up into him who is the Head, that is, Christ. [16]From him the whole body, joined and held together by every supporting ligament, grows and builds itself up in love, as each part does its work.

According to verse 7, who receives spiritual gifts?

What gifts do you find listed in verse 11?

This passage contains two clues about the purpose of spiritual gifts. Look at verses 12 and 16. What do you find there about the purpose of spiritual gifts?

What does this passage have to say about what happens when we use our spiritual gifts?

1 Peter 4:10-11

> [10]*Each one should use whatever gift he has received to serve others, faithfully administering God's grace in its various forms.* [11]*If anyone speaks, he should do it as one speaking the very words of God. If anyone serves, he should do it with the strength God provides, so that in all things God may be praised through Jesus Christ. To him be the glory and the power for ever and ever. Amen.*

According to verse 10, who receives spiritual gifts?

Verse 11 lists two methods for using the gifts, actually how you use them. What are these?

Search the Scriptures

Look through the Bible passages from this chapter and fill in the white blanks in the chart on the next page. Write the words directly from Scripture; don't paraphrase.

Do you see the patterns? First, over and over again Scripture says, *each one* has received a spiritual gift. That means that every Christian receives at least one gift. So just in case you were thinking that you weren't home the day God handed out spiritual gifts, you can forget that right now. As a child of God, you *do* have a spiritual gift. Gifts are also not age or gender specific. Gifts may change or develop, and certain gifts become more obvious as we mature in our faith.

Second, we see a pattern in the purpose of the gifts. Notice how Scripture never says that that spiritual gifts are our own to keep for our own pleasure or benefit. Instead, in each passage, the Bible tells us that our gifts are to be used to serve one another, to build up the church, or to glorify God. That means that we cannot keep them to ourselves. God expects us to use our gifts!

Discovering and using our gifts isn't only a blessing to others, though. Doing so gives us a sense of meaning and purpose as well as fulfillment, knowing that we are living into God's plan for our lives.

But how do we find out what gifts we have? That process can begin in a number of ways. One way is to complete a spiritual gifts assessment, like the one in Chapter 2. Keep in mind that the assessment is just a tool. The evidence is when you use a gift and see results, either reflected in the effectiveness of your efforts or confirmed by the comments of your fellow believers that you have done something well.

In the next chapter, you'll have an opportunity to discover your own gifts; and we'll take a closer look at the individual gifts to gain an understanding of what they are and what purpose they each serve in the body of Christ.

Verse	Who receives the gifts?	What is the purpose of the gifts?
Romans 12:6		
1 Corinthians 12:7		
Ephesians 4:7		
Ephesians 4:12		
1 Peter 4:10		
1 Peter 4:11		

Chapter 2: Spiritual Gifts Discovery

Like good stewards of the manifold grace of God, serve one another with whatever gift each of you has received. (1 Peter 4:10)

Spiritual Gifts Discovery Tool

The "S" in S.T.R.I.D.E. stands for *spiritual* gifts. The following is a list of 80 statements. Answer based on how true these statements are of your life experiences, both past and present, not how you wish they were. There are no right or wrong answers—just realistic responses that will be different for each person. Remember that God's choice of gifts for you is in harmony with God's perfect plan and will for your life.

Record your answer on the line next to each statement. When you are finished, transfer your responses onto the response form on page 18. Score each one as follows:

4—Very true of me, consistently
3—Frequently true of me
2—Occasionally true of me
1—Infrequently true of me
0—Rarely or never true of me

_____ 1. I tend to be organized and am detail-oriented when working on projects or homework.

_____ 2. I would enjoy being a part of a mission team in a foreign country or serving people from a diverse culture.

_____ 3. I can sense when someone's motives or intentions go against God's ideas.

_____ 4. I have talents as a singer, artist, writer, or musician that I'd like to use to encourage people in their faith.

_____ 5. I am open about my faith, and I look for opportunities to talk with others about my faith.

_____ 6. I am absolutely sure that God will keep God's promises.

_____ 7. I enjoy sharing my material possessions with others.

_____ 8. I regularly pray for healing on behalf of others and believe that God can answer those prayers in miraculous ways.

_____ 9. I am happy doing the behind-the-scenes work at church.

_____10. I enjoy reading and studying my Bible in depth.

_____11. People often come to me, looking for help or direction.

_____12. My heart hurts when I see people who are hurting, and I am moved to action.

_____13. I am concerned whether the people I know are growing spiritually.

_____14. I confront people who have acted out against their faith and encourage them to turn back to God.

_____15. I am able to explain Bible verses in ways that others can understand and relate to their lives.

_____16. People often ask me for advice about difficult decisions or situations.

_____17. I enjoy helping plan and organize events or projects.

_____18. I am good at juggling many tasks and projects at once and doing them all well.

_____19. I know when something I hear or read is not in line with God's Word.

_____20. I am able to gently guide people in a way that helps them remain faithful to God.

_____21. I like to invite people to come to church or youth group with me.

_____22. I don't get overly discouraged when bad things happen, because I know that God is in control.

_____23. I give a significant portion of my time and any money I earn to charitable causes.

_____24. I feel prompted to pray for people by name who are in need and are hurting.

_____25. I enjoy using my talents and skills to help in a variety of ways around the church.

_____26. When someone is confused, I show him or her a Bible passage to help make things clear.

_____27. I inspire other people to volunteer in church, and I support their work when they do.

_____28. I want to follow Jesus' example of compassion by helping people in need.

_____29. I develop friendships with others and encourage them in their faith walk.

_____30. I see things in the world that are opposed to God's will, and I feel led to expose them.

_____31. I enjoy preparing and organizing material so that I can teach it to others.

_____32. Somehow I am able to come up with simple solutions to complex situations.

_____33. I easily understand and follow the steps needed to achieve a goal.

_____34. I like to encourage others to assume leadership roles.

_____35. I have been able to get individuals and groups back on track with God's Word.

_____36. I bring comfort to people through sharing God's promises.

_____37. I can share the gospel in ways that are helpful to people.

_____38. I am able to encourage individuals or groups to keep going when they are thinking about giving up.

_____39. When I see someone in need, I share whatever I have.

_____40. I believe that God answers my prayers and heals the people I pray for.

_____41. I often help out around the church by doing whatever needs to be done.

_____42. I like to tell others what I have learned through reading and studying the Bible.

_____43. I encourage others to develop their skills and abilities.

_____44. I enjoy visiting people who are sick or lonely to bring them a little cheer.

_____45. I enjoy teaching individuals and groups over extended periods of time.

_____46. I get the urge to talk about the will of God in order to encourage or guide people.

_____47. Whenever I learn something new, I can't wait to talk with others about the new knowledge.

_____48. I sometimes make difficult situations easier to understand and can help point others toward God for answers.

_____49. I can figure out exactly what it will take for a project to run smoothly.

_____50. I am drawn to tell about my faith in places in settings where there are non-believers.

_____51. I sometimes sense the presence of evil.

_____52. People are likely to make more godly decisions or changes in their lives after spending time with me.

_____53. I intentionally develop relationships with non-believers for the purpose of sharing my faith.

_____54. I believe that God listens to and answers all prayers.

_____55. I believe that God has blessed me so that I can be a blessing to others.

_____56. I am drawn to worship experiences where prayers and anointing for healing are experienced.

_____57. I enjoy providing practical help to meet ministry needs.

_____58. I am able to explain an understanding of God and the Bible that helps others grow in faith.

_____59. I often find myself in a leadership role.

_____60. I am a good listener, and people often talk to me about their troubles.

_____61. I feel the responsibility of caring for the people I teach about God and God's Word.

_____62. I am often led to point out destructive behaviors and help get others back on a right path.

_____63. People often thank me for helping them better understand the Bible or materials from a Bible study.

_____64. I am able to share words and insights that bring peaceful solutions to problems.

_____65. I like to work with issues involving systems, structure, and procedures.

_____66. I feel compelled to tell about the gospel, and I spend time in prayer and God's Word to prepare myself.

_____67. I have experienced, personally and in groups, guidance from the Holy Spirit in answer to a time of prayer.

_____68. I am led to encourage people in their faith through serving.

_____69. I am comfortable using prayer and the Bible to lead people to faith in Jesus.

_____70. I approach challenges with confidence when I know that I am doing what God wants me to do.

_____71. Everything I have is a gift from God, and I seek out ways to share those gifts with others.

_____72. People have told me about times that they have experienced God's healing touch because of my prayers on their behalf.

_____73. Serving God through simple tasks is something I like to do.

_____74. God sometimes gives me a special understanding about the Bible that helps me explain it to others in a way that helps them understand.

_____75. I tend to have a "big picture" perspective and can help others see the vision in a way that is understandable and motivating.

_____76. I can serve people in need in a way that protects their dignity.

_____77. I am not only interested in teaching people about God, but I also care a lot about the people I teach.

_____78. A Bible verse will sometimes come to my mind in situations where people need direction or encouragement.

_____79. I look for opportunities to tell about what I have learned about the Bible.

_____80. God provides me with spiritual thoughts and words to help make things clear for other people.

Total your responses across, then transfer the totals to the corresponding letter on page 19.

TOTAL

1____	17____	33____	49____	65____	A _____
2____	18____	34____	50____	66____	B _____
3____	19____	35____	51____	67____	C _____
4____	20____	36____	52____	68____	D _____
5____	21____	37____	53____	69____	E _____
6____	22____	38____	54____	70____	F _____
7____	23____	39____	55____	71____	G _____
8____	24____	40____	56____	72____	H _____
9____	25____	41____	57____	73____	I _____
10____	26____	42____	58____	74____	J _____
11____	27____	43____	59____	75____	K _____
12____	28____	44____	60____	76____	L _____
13____	29____	45____	61____	77____	M _____
14____	30____	46____	62____	78____	N _____
15____	31____	47____	63____	79____	O _____
16____	32____	48____	64____	80____	P _____

Spiritual Gifts		Scores From Page 18
A.	Organizational Leadership	_____
B.	Apostleship	_____
C.	Recognizing What's of God	_____
D.	Encouragement	_____
E.	Evangelism	_____
F.	Faith	_____
G.	Generosity	_____
H.	Healing	_____
I.	Helping	_____
J.	Studying the Bible	_____
K.	Motivational Leadership	_____
L.	Mercy & Compassion	_____
M.	Nurturing Others' Growth	_____
N.	Prophecy	_____
O.	Teaching	_____
P.	Speaking God's Truth	_____

My top three gifts, according to my scores, are

1. _____

2. _____

3. _____

Turn to "This Is Who I Am," on page 56; and write these three gifts in the space provided.

Chapter 3: Spiritual Gifts Defined

Like good stewards of the manifold grace of God, serve one another with whatever gift each of you has received. (1 Peter 4:10)

The Spiritual Gifts Discovery Tool, in Chapter 2, helped you narrow down your possible gifts from the sixteen gifts listed. You have prayerfully considered the questions within the tool and have identified your top three spiritual gifts. Now that you have a list of three of the gifts God has given you, you'll probably want to know more about what spiritual gifts are.

Spiritual gifts are special abilities given to every Christian, by the grace of God, through the Holy Spirit, to be used to serve and strengthen one another and to glorify God.

In a nutshell, spiritual gifts are

- ✧ abilities given by God (not something you've learned);
- ✧ given to every Christian (yes, even YOU!);
- ✧ given through the grace of God (not something you've earned);
- ✧ given by the Holy Spirit (who chooses which gifts you receive);
- ✧ used to serve and strengthen one another (to build one another up, not yourself); and
- ✧ used to glorify God (for God's purposes, to God's glory).

So how can you be sure that you really have the three identified spiritual gifts? And what difference could that make in your life?

Confirmation of your spiritual gifts—that feeling of "Yes, this is right for me"—can come in a variety of ways:

- ✧ You will be drawn to use your spiritual gift(s). (You are drawn to do what God has equipped you to do.)
- ✧ Others will recognize that gift in you. (Others benefit.)
- ✧ You will be comfortable serving in your area of spiritual giftedness. (But you may still have butterflies in your stomach when you use your gift.)

✧ You will be effective when you use that gift. (God gets the glory, though, not you.)

Take a deep breath. It's time to continue our journey. This is where it gets really exciting, since our path is leading us to a deeper understanding of each of the spiritual gifts. In the next section, you'll find a list of sixteen of the spiritual gifts referred to in the Bible. Take time to research what the Bible says about the three gifts on which you received the highest scores. Look up the Bible passages listed in this chapter for those gifts, and write down your notes and reflections.

Apostleship

From the Greek word *apostolos,* which means "a delegate, a special ambassador of the gospel, a messenger."

A person with this gift is eager to bring the gospel to those who have never heard it. He or she may share the Good News when preaching the Word, teaching others to live as Jesus taught us to live, and modeling a Christian life. A person with the gift of apostleship will creatively find ways to reach persons for whom the teachings of Jesus may be new. He or she may enjoy doing so in places with different or diverse cultures or may be especially drawn to local or foreign mission work.

Scripture References: Acts 6:2-4; Ephesians 4:11-13; 2 Peter 3:2

A Contemporary Example

Hal is a quiet, understated guy. As one friend says, "I knew right away that there was something different about him, a peace I couldn't quite figure out. When I knew him better, I realized that his faith made a big difference in his life. He never pushed it on me; but little by little, I learned a lot about God and Jesus through what he said and who he was."

Questions to Consider

❍ Do you know persons who have the gift of apostleship?

❍ How can you encourage these persons as they exercise this spiritual gift?

❍ Do you believe that you have the gift of apostleship? If so, what are some ways you might share the good news about Jesus?

❍ Who do you know who doesn't know or understand who Jesus Christ was and why he came to earth?

❍ In what ways can you offer the gift of apostleship to friends, family, classmates?

Helping

From the Greek word *diakonia*, which means "service, ministry, aid, relief."

A person with this gift receives spiritual satisfaction from doing everyday, necessary tasks; he or she may prefer to work quietly and without public recognition. When a need arises, the helper often takes care of it without being asked.

Scripture References: Acts 24:23; Philippians 2:25-30; 2 Timothy 4:11; Hebrews 6:10

A Contemporary Example

Akeesha is one of those always-there-when-you-need-them people. She figures out what needs to be done and does it quietly. Most people don't even know all she does setting up for youth group meetings, making phone calls, or cleaning up after a meal. And that's fine with her.

Questions to Consider

❍ Do you know persons who have the gift of helping?

❍ How can you encourage these persons as they exercise this gift?

❍ Do you believe that you have the gift of helping? If so, where in your church community can you be of service?

❍ In what ways can you offer this gift to friends, family, classmates?

Recognizing What Is of God

From the Greek word *diakrisis*, which means "discerning, judicial estimation."

A person with this gift can usually rely on instincts or first impressions to tell when a person or message is deceptive or inconsistent with biblical truths. He or she recognizes what is of God and what is not of God and is able to judge with mercy and understanding, instead of with condemnation.

Scripture References: Acts 13:8-12; Acts 17:11; 2 Corinthians 11:13-15; 1 John 4:1

A Contemporary Example

Carlos felt that there was something wrong in the new girl's story. Carlos talked with her, listened carefully, and asked a few probing questions. His instinct told him that she wasn't being totally truthful. When he told her, "You can be straight with me," she opened up and told him the truth of who she was.

Questions to Consider

❍ Do you know persons whose gift is recognizing what is "of God"?

❍ How can you encourage these persons as they exercise this gift?

❍ Do you believe that you have the gift of recognizing what is "of God"? If so, how can you be loving and understanding in situations that you sense are not "of God"?

❍ In what ways can you offer this gift to friends, family, classmates?

Evangelism

From the Greek word *euaggelistes*, which means "a preacher of the gospel."

A person with this gift speaks comfortably about his or her faith; even nonbelievers are drawn into this circle of comfort. These people enjoy many friendships outside of their Christian community. He or she enjoys helping others see how Christianity can fulfill their needs.

Scripture References: Luke 9:6; Acts 5:42; 8:26-40; 16:6-10

A Contemporary Example

Grace loves to share her faith with other people. People who know her speak of how she can fervently talk about what Jesus means in her life, without, as one friend says, "pushing her ideas down your throat." Grace is comfortable talking about youth group and prayer and can go to church even with people who are part of other faith communities or have no connection to a church or synagogue.

Questions to Consider

❍ Do you know persons with the gift of evangelism?

❍ How can you encourage these persons as they exercise this gift?

❍ Do you believe that you have the gift of evangelism? If so, what persons do you know who might benefit from hearing the good news?

❍ In what ways can you offer this gift to friends, family, classmates?

Encouragement

From the Greek word *paraklesis,* which means "comfort, solace, encouragement."

A person with this gift encourages others to remain faithful, even in the midst of struggles. Encouragement may take many forms and can be done through personal relationships, music, writings, intercessory prayer, and speaking, to name a few. The encourager can see positive traits or aspects that other persons overlook, and often have more faith in other persons than they have in themselves.

Scripture References: Acts 14:22; 15:31-33; 20:1-2; 2 Timothy 4:2

A Contemporary Example

Su-Lin is a magnet for other youth who are hurting, confused, or just need a shoulder to lean on. "I try to be a good friend," she explains. "Sometimes she gives me ideas of how to handle a sticky situation," one classmate says. "She might promise to pray for me. I always feel better after talking to Su-Lin."

Questions to Consider

○ Do you know persons who have the gift of encouragement?

○ How can you encourage these persons as they exercise this gift?

○ Do you believe that you have the gift of encouragement? If so, what are ways you have encouraged others?

○ In what ways can you offer this gift to friends, family, classmates?

Faith

From the Greek word *pistis,* which means "faith in God, moral conviction, assurance."

A person with this gift, by works and by words, shows others that God is faithful to God's promises. Even in the face of barriers that overwhelm others, a person with this gift simply knows that God is present and active in his or her life.

Scripture References: Matthew 9:2, 22; Acts 14:22; Ephesians 2:8-9; 1 Timothy 6:11

A Contemporary Example

When James was a junior, a surfing accident put him in a wheelchair for the rest of his life. Before the school year ended he was back at school and, with a friend's help, attended all of his classes. Even though the accident meant that he would never play soccer again, he volunteered to be the team manager his senior year. On the back of his wheelchair is a poster that says, "With God, all things are possible."

Questions to Consider

○ Do you know persons who have the gift of faith?

○ How can you encourage these persons as they exercise this gift?

○ Do you believe that you have the gift of faith? If so, how do others know that you have this gift?

○ In what ways can you offer this gift to friends, family, classmates?

Generosity

From the Greek word *metadidomi,* which means "to give over, share, impart."

A person with this gift gives freely and joyfully of himself or herself and his or her material wealth. He or she usually manages finances well, may have a special ability to make money, and tends to have a frugal lifestyle. Instead of asking, "How much money do I give to God?" a giver asks, "How much of God's money do I keep?"

Scripture References: Luke 3:11; Romans 12:8; 1 Thessalonians 2:8

A Contemporary Example

Sam had no trouble collecting funds for the school Aids Research Drive. People could see that he believed in the cause, and he promised to match their contributions with money he earned as a lifeguard. Sure, he could have spent the money on new CDs or a round of golf; but Sam's focus was on fundraising and helping people with HIV/AIDS.

Questions to Consider

○ Do you know persons who have the gift of generosity?

○ How can you encourage these persons as they exercise this gift?

○ Do you believe you have the gift of generosity? If so, what are some examples of your previous generosity?

○ In what ways can you offer this gift to friends, family, classmates?

Healing

From the Greek words *charismas,* which means "a spiritual endowment," and *iama,* which means "cures, healings."

A person with this gift listens skillfully as he or she seeks God's guidance to learn the needs of the sick. His or her tools include prayer, touch, and spoken words. Someone with the gift of healing believes that God can cure and that prayer can overcome any negative forces at work. The healer believes that God heals bodies, minds, spirits, and relationships.

Scripture References: Matthew 4:23; Luke 9:11; Acts 4:28-30; 10:38

A Contemporary Example

Ever since Donello was in first grade, she has wanted to be a doctor. Although she doesn't yet have the knowledge or skill to practice medicine, she likes to volunteer at a local hospital in the pediatric ward. "I know that I make the children happy when I visit," she says. "And that helps them get better faster."

Questions to Consider

○ Do you know persons who have the gift of healing?

○ How can you encourage these persons as they exercise this gift?

○ Do you believe that you have the gift of healing? If so, what situations have called forth this gift in the past?

○ In what ways can you offer this gift to friends, family, classmates?

Organizational Leadership

From the Greek word *kubernesis*, which means "to steer or guide."

A person with this gift handles details carefully and thoroughly. He or she is skilled in determining priorities and in planning and directing the steps needed to achieve a goal. He or she is frustrated with disorder and is uncomfortable with inefficiency. This God-given ability helps him or her organize and manage information, people, events and resources to make projects happen.

Scripture References: Acts 6:1-7; 1 Corinthians 12:28; Titus 1:5

A Contemporary Example

Hannah loves lists. Scratching through the tasks she has accomplished on her "to do" list gives her great pleasure. "If I need something done thoroughly, I ask Hannah," her youth leader says. "She has an uncanny way of figuring out what needs to be done when, whether we're planning a car wash or a mission trip. In her quiet way she keeps the rest of us on track."

Questions to Consider

❍ Do you know persons who have the gift of organizational leadership?

❍ How can you encourage these persons as they exercise this gift?

❍ Do you believe that you have the gift of organizational leadership? If so, how have you practiced this gift in the past?

❍ In what ways can you offer this gift to friends, family, classmates?

Motivational Leadership

From the Greek word *proistemi*, which means "to preside, maintain, be over."

A person with this gift is a visionary who inspires others to work together to make the vision a reality. He or she takes responsibility for setting and achieving goals and steps in where there is a lack of direction. A motivator builds a team of talented persons and empowers them.

Scripture References: John 13:12-17; Philippians 3:17-21; Hebrews 13:7, 17

A Contemporary Example

A.J. is president of his church youth group, is vice-president of his school's student council, and serves on his church leadership committee. People like to be around A.J. because he makes them feel like they are an important part of any team project. Whether he's running a planning meeting or recruiting others to help with a spaghetti dinner, A.J. engages his peers in a way that inspires them to give their best effort for the group.

Questions to Consider

❍ Do you know persons who have the gift of motivational leadership?

❍ How can you encourage these persons as they exercise this gift?

❍ Do you believe that you have this gift? If so, whom do you motivate?

❍ In what ways can you offer this gift to friends, family, classmates?

Mercy and Compassion

From the Greek word *eleeo*, which means "to have compassion, to have mercy on."

A person with this gift is called to reach out to someone who is hurt or rejected. He or she feels fulfilled when showing others that God loves them. This gift is compassion moved to action.

Scripture References: Matthew 9:36; Luke 10:30-37; Colossians 3:12-15

A Contemporary Example

Yaíma brings home stray pets and often befriends other youth who usually stand on the fringes of groups. She likes to volunteer at an inner-city soup kitchen and looks forward to the CROP Hunger Walk* each year, when she raises money for hunger relief. "It just makes me feel good," Yaíma explains.

Questions to Consider

❍ Do you know persons who have the gift of mercy and compassion?

❍ How can you encourage these persons as they exercise this gift?

❍ Do you believe that you have the gift of mercy and compassion? If so, what individuals, groups or causes have captured your heart?

❍ In what ways can you offer this gift to friends, family, classmates?

* To learn about how to participate in a CROP Hunger Walk, go to *www.cropwalk.org*.

Nurturing Others' Growth

From the Greek words *poimen*, which means "a shepherd," and *didaskalos*, which means "teacher."

A person with this gift enjoys working with groups of people and nurturing their growth over an extended period of time. The nurturer guides, protects, and cares for other Christians as they experience spiritual growth.

Scripture References: Jeremiah 3:15; 7:16; Ezekiel 34; John 10:1-16; Ephesians 4:11-16; 1 Peter 5:1-4

A Contemporary Example

Having volunteered at the preschool where his mother worked since he was in elementary school, Aneal recently added Sunday school teacher to his resume. "I love teaching the kids about God," he says. "Being with them as they learn new Bible stories, discussing how they can pray for other people, teaching them church songs I've loved since I was little means a lot to me."

Questions to Consider

O Do you know persons whose gift is nurturing others' growth?

O How can you encourage them as they exercise this spiritual gift?

O Do you believe that you have the gift of nurturing others' growth? If so, whom are you currently nurturing in his or her faith?

O In what ways can you offer this gift to friends, family, classmates?

Prophecy

From the Greek word *propheteuo,* which means "speak under inspiration."

A person with this gift listens carefully to God for what God wants him or her to say. A prophet warns others of the immediate or future consequences of not accepting God's truths. He or she can see sin or deception that others overlook. Prophecy means proclaiming God's truth in a relevant way.

Scripture References: 1 Corinthians 13:2; 14:3; Ephesians 4:11-13; Revelation 19:10

A Contemporary Example

Josh is unafraid to speak up when he sees injustice or something wrong. He'll step in to stop a fight without worrying about getting hurt. He confronts racist or sexist joke-tellers and wears a WWJD? (What Would Jesus Do?) bracelet. "Not everyone wants to hear what he says," one friend admits. "But we all respect him and how strong he can be."

Questions to Consider

❍ Do you know persons who have the gift of prophecy?

❍ How can you encourage them as they exercise this gift?

❍ Do you believe that you have the gift of prophecy? If so, what have been some of the messages you've felt called to share?

❍ In what ways can you offer this gift to friends, family, classmates?

Teaching

From the Greek word *didaskalias*, which means "instruction, the act of imparting the truth."

A person with this gift enjoys studying the Bible and inspires listeners to greater obedience to God's Word. He or she not only communicates the facts, but also shows how Scripture applies to everyday life. The teacher prepares through study and reflection and pays close attention to detail.

Scripture References: Matthew 28:19-20; Colossians 1:28; 1 Timothy 6:3-5; Titus 1:7-11; James 3:1

A Contemporary Example

Jules was nervous the first time he led his youth group in devotions; but once he was up front, his words surprised even him. "I had prepared; but once I got started, I thought of other things I had read that also went along with what I was trying to say. My nervousness left, and I felt focused on helping the group understand how the psalm made sense for us." Others in his group were impressed with his preparation and clarity.

Questions to Consider

❍ Do you know persons who have the gift of teaching?

❍ How can you encourage them as they exercise this gift?

❍ Do you believe that you have the gift of teaching? If so, where have you used this gift so far?

❍ In what ways can you offer this gift to friends, family, classmates?

Studying the Bible

From the Greek words *logos*, which means "something said, communication," and *gnosis*, which means "knowledge."

A person with this gift enjoys studying the Bible and other sources to gain facts, insights, and truths. He or she understands, organizes, and effectively uses God-given insight on this information to bring other people closer to God.

Scripture References: Proverbs 1:7; Jeremiah 3:15; Malachi 2:7, 2; Romans 10:2-3; 2 Peter 1:2-11

A Contemporary Example

"Brandi can think of a Bible verse for every situation," one friend says. "She doesn't come across as corny, because she's so sincere. She remembers things that none of the rest of us have even heard of; and amazingly, what she says usually makes sense for whatever's going on."

Questions to Consider

○ Do you know persons who have the gift of studying the Bible?

○ How can you encourage them as they exercise this gift?

○ Do you believe that you have the gift of studying the Bible? If so, how can you nurture that gift? Are there classes you can take to learn more?

○ In what ways can you offer this gift to friends, family, classmates?

Speaking God's Truth

From the Greek words *logos*, meaning "something said, communication," and *sophia*, meaning "wisdom."

A person with this gift has an ability to understand and live God's will. He or she speaks God's truth as found in Scripture as a way to provide direction to people who are struggling with which way they should go.

Scripture References: Colossians 1:9-12, 28; 2:3; 3:16; James 3:13.

A Contemporary Example

"It doesn't matter whether Hailey's talking about a track meet or the school prom," her pastor says. "She sees everything from her perspective as a Christian." Her best friend agrees: "I get so confused at times, but Hailey always asks questions or makes comments that remind me to focus on how God wants me to live. Sometimes that makes my decisions easier."

Questions to Consider

❍ Do you know persons who have the gift of speaking God's truth?

❍ How can you encourage them as they exercise this gift?

❍ Do you believe that you have the gift of speaking God's truth? If so, how have you previously used this gift?

❍ In what ways can you offer this gift to friends, family, classmates?

Appreciate the Benefits

❍ What are the benefits of discovering, developing, and using your spiritual gifts?

Personal Benefits

- You will have a better understanding of God's purpose for your life. God gives each person unique gifts to fulfill God's specific plan.
- Your relationship with God will grow and mature. As you minister to others and see the difference God makes in their lives through you, your relationship with God will deepen.
- Your life and work will be more effective and fulfilling. For example, if you have a passion for children and the gift of teaching, you might really enjoy being an effective Sunday school teacher. Why not give it a try?

Kingdom Benefits

God is glorified, and God's people are built up in the church and world as everyone uses his or her individual, unique gifts.

Church Benefits

Imagine a church where everyone knows his or her unique gifts. Persons with the gift of helping help, persons with the gift of mercy reach out to those who are suffering, and so forth. The church ministry is effective with ministries that grow spiritually. When you use your gifts in service to others, you see God at work through you, changing lives and changing the world one person at a time.

Other Gifts

In addition to the sixteen spiritual gifts listed in this chapter, the Bible talks about three other possible spiritual gifts. These gifts are more specific to the early church, and scholars debate whether anyone today even has these gifts. One thing is for sure about them: They don't lend themselves to specific ministries in the church. For that reason, we have not included them in this study. To discover more about these gifts, read the suggested Scripture passages. If you think that you may have one of these divine gifts, set up time to further explore this gift with your pastor or youth leader.

Performing Miracles

A person with this gift performs miracles for the purpose of getting attention to point out God's power. The performance of these miracles leads to listening, following, and believing in the message by those who witness the miracles.

Scripture References: John 2:11; 6:2; Acts 2:22; 8:6, 13; Hebrews 2:4

Speaking in Tongues

A person with this gift is able to speak a message from God in a language that he or she has not naturally learned. This gift of tongues is a sign to believers, showing the power and glory of God.

Scripture References: Acts 2:11; 1 Corinthians 14

Interpreting Tongues

A person with this gift is able to translate the message of someone speaking in tongues. His or her ability to interpret the gift of tongues builds up the church as hearers understand God's message.

Scripture References: 1 Corinthians 12:10; 14

Chapter 4: Talents and Resources

I appeal to you therefore, brothers and sisters, by the mercies of God, to present your bodies as a living sacrifice, holy and acceptable to God, which is your spiritual worship. (Romans 12:1)

The "T" in S.T.R.I.D.E. stands for our *talents*—both God given and acquired. Every person is born with natural talents, whether for athletics, music, arithmetic, mechanics, or something else altogether. Talents are those abilities that seem to come naturally. See whether you can identify the talents of the following people:

Tiger Woods _____

Beyoncé Knowles _____

Bill Gates _____

J.K. Rowling_____

Sometimes people confuse talents with spiritual gifts. Talents and spiritual gifts can seem very similar because both refer to an exceptional ability to do something. Natural abilities may mirror gifts, but there are some differences. Spiritual gifts are given to Christians, while every person (Christian or not) is born with natural talents. Talents are sometimes used to benefit others, but they can also be used in a way that benefits only the individual. Spiritual gifts are used to glorify God and to serve others.

What about you? What abilities come naturally to you?

My Talents and Abilities

The real me (*check all that apply*):

____ I don't think that I have many talents/abilities, or much to offer God.

____ Other people seem to have more to offer God than I do.

____ I'm not sure how my talents work with my spiritual gifts.

____ I have a few natural abilities, which I try to use for God's glory.

____ I know that God can and will use me to serve others.

____ I am blessed with many talents, which I try to use for God's glory.

____ I wish that I knew more ways to use my gifts in God's service.

One way to distinguish whether an ability is a talent or a spiritual gift is to consider the purpose and the results. Does the ability serve others? Does the ability glorify God? Spiritual gifts will have a "yes" answer to both of these questions.

Acquired skills and expertise can be used to serve others and glorify God as well. Public speaking and expertise in computer, graphic arts, or audio-video technology can all have a place serving within the body of Christ.

Sometimes people use their natural talents or acquired skills in concert with their spiritual gifts. Someone with a great singing voice may use that musical talent in church worship or in leading a children's choir. The person who is skilled in audio-video technology may help out with worship or teaching opportunities at church. Computer skills might be used to produce a newsletter, to create a youth group or church website, or to send e-mails.

God can also transform our natural talents into spiritual gifts. For instance, God may elevate and amplify someone's natural leadership to the point of a spiritual gift when that person enters into a relationship with Jesus Christ.

Some jobs or tasks cannot be completed without help from God. We have to be open to let God work through us for great things to happen. In the Bible, when the Moabites, Ammonites, and some Meunites came to make war against King Jehoshaphat and the Israelites (2 Chronicles 20), Jehoshaphat called upon the Lord for help. God answered him saying, "Do not fear or be dismayed at this great multitude; for the battle is not yours but God's" (2 Chronicles 20:15, NRSV). The same is true for us today as we serve God. We need to get out of the way and let the Holy Spirit work through us. We are only God's instruments.

Yvonne, co-author of this study, agreed to teach this spiritual gifts discovery course, based on her past experience speaking in front of groups. She knew the material and thought that she could handle teaching, on the merit of her own abilities; so she was surprised when the first two classes didn't go well. One evening after class, she went home in tears and prayed to God: "I can't do this. I need your help. Next week, I'll show up; but you'll have to teach the class. If you don't want me doing this, I'll know."

Amazingly, the next week it was as though the Holy Spirit did teach the class. Yvonne's speaking ability was used; but the difference was that now she was willing to allow the Holy Spirit to work through her, instead of relying on her own abilities.

Which of your natural talents or acquired skills could God use for God's purposes?

(Write these on page 56.)

We need to recognize that all abilities come from God. In that sense, they are gifts and can be dedicated to God's work. What makes spiritual gifts distinct is that God owns the results. God gets the credit because what is accomplished is beyond our own abilities.

In the Bible passage that opens this chapter, Paul instructs us to "present [our] bodies as a living sacrifice." That includes our whole selves—our gifts, our talents, our dreams, our individual styles, and our resources.

Resources

You did not choose me but I chose you. And I appointed you to go and bear fruit, fruit that will last, so that the Father will give you whatever you ask him in my name." (John 15:16, NRSV)

The "R" in S.T.R.I.D.E. stands for *resources*. When we think of resources, most of us usually think of financial resources. These are certainly part of our resource pool, but there is so much more. Our resources include

- our finances;
- our time;
- our material possessions;
- our contacts (friends, family, teachers, acquaintances);
- our hobbies; and
- other aspects of our lives personal to each one of us.

Take time to think about your own life. What resources are available to you? Jot down your ideas on the next page.

Resources in My Life

My support system of family and friends:

My acquaintance network:

My access to financial resources (through parents, savings, or a job):

My material possessions:

My available time:

My hobbies:

Other things unique to my life that might be resources:

(*Write some of your key resources on page 56.*)

There is an old saying that goes something like this: "I've never seen a hearse towing a U-Haul trailer behind it." The meaning is pretty clear—you can't take it with you. The good news is that Jesus taught us that you can't take it with you, but you can send it on ahead. As Jesus said in Matthew 6:19-21:

> "*Do not store up for yourselves treasures on earth, where moth and rust consume and where thieves break in and steal; but store up for yourselves treasures in heaven, where neither moth nor rust consumes and where thieves do not break in and steal. For where your treasure is, there your heart will be also.*" (NRSV)

Christ instructed us to invest in things of eternal value: God and people. How do we invest in these? By being good stewards of (taking good care of) our resources.

Jesus told a wonderful story, or parable, that explains the stewardship of our resources. It is often called the parable of the talents, since talents were the name of a type of money used in Jesus' time.

Parable of the Talents (Matthew 25:14-30)

[14]"Again, it will be like a man going on a journey, who called his servants and entrusted his property to them. [15]To one he gave five talents[a] of money, to another two talents, and to another one talent, each according to his ability. Then he went on his journey. [16]The man who had received the five talents went at once and put his money to work and gained five more. [17]So also, the one with the two talents gained two more. [18]But the man who had received the one talent went off, dug a hole in the ground and hid his master's money.

[19]"After a long time the master of those servants returned and settled accounts with them. [20]The man who had received the five talents brought the other five. 'Master,' he said, 'you entrusted me with five talents. See, I have gained five more.'

[21]"His master replied, 'Well done, good and faithful servant! You have been faithful with a few things; I will put you in charge of many things. Come and share your master's happiness!'

[22]"The man with the two talents also came. 'Master,' he said, 'you entrusted me with two talents; see, I have gained two more.'

[23]"His master replied, 'Well done, good and faithful servant! You have been faithful with a few things; I will put you in charge of many things. Come and share your master's happiness!'

[24]"Then the man who had received the one talent came. 'Master,' he said, 'I knew that you are a hard man, harvesting where you have not sown and gathering where you have not scattered seed. [25]So I was afraid and went out and hid your talent in the ground. See, here is what belongs to you.'

[26]"His master replied, 'You wicked, lazy servant! So you knew that I harvest where I have not sown and gather where I have not scattered seed? [27]Well then, you should have put my money on deposit with the bankers, so that when I returned I would have received it back with interest.

[28]" 'Take the talent from him and give it to the one who has the ten talents. [29]For everyone who has will be given more, and he will have an abundance. Whoever does not have, even what he has will be taken from him. [30]And throw that worthless servant outside, into the darkness, where there will be weeping and gnashing of teeth.'" (NIV)

For me, the point of this story of the three servants is. . .

If I think of the talent in this story as being the sum of all my resources (not just money), I am more like

____A. the servant with one talent, who hid the master's money in a hole in the ground;

____B. the servant who doubled his master's gift;

____C. the servant who had the most talents and made even more by his work; or

____D. I'm not sure.

Have you ever heard the saying "From those to whom much is given, much will be expected"? That's the message of this parable:

- All that we have is from God.

- What we have is not ours to keep for ourselves (or to hide in a hole in the ground!) but is ours to use while we're here on earth.

- We are caretakers, or stewards, of all that we have.

How can I use my resources for God?

Investing in things that are eternal also includes setting priorities based on our values and then living by those priorities. If family time is a priority, you make time to hang out with your family. If sharing your life in Christ with others is a priority, you attend worship, Sunday school, youth group. If helping other people matters to you, you find ways to volunteer and make a difference in another person's life.

What are the priorities of my life?

Does the way I spend my time reflect my priorities? If so, how?

Chapter 5: Individuality

There is one body and one Spirit, just as you were called to the one hope of your calling, one Lord, one faith, one baptism, one God and Father of all, who is above all and through all and in all.

But each of us was given grace according to the measure of Christ's gift. (Ephesians 4:4-7)

No two snowflakes are alike. No two people are alike. That means that in all of God's creation, there is no one else like you. You are a genuine, one-of-a-kind original, with a style all your own. God created you to be unique. Hitting our S.T.R.I.D.E. means recognizing and celebrating our *individuality*—that's what the "I" reminds us of.

So how does that uniqueness influence the ways in which we serve God?

❖ Our style affects the way we think.
❖ Our style affects the way we expend and receive energy.
❖ Our style affects the way we organize our work.
❖ Our style affects the way we interact with other people.

A variety of tools help people determine their style or personality type. For simplicity's sake, we're going to focus on two key components of individuality that have the most direct impact on our service: 1) personality type and 2) the environment in which we prefer to work. We'll learn about introverted and extroverted personalities, and then focus on whether you prefer a flexible or stable environment. By the time we're done, you'll know more about yourself and how you function in the world. This information should help you in your service to God, in your work at school, and in other aspects of your life.

Can we determine a person's style just by watching him or her? Not necessarily. For instance, Carmen speaks quite well in front of groups and seems to make small talk with ease. She introduces herself to new people and makes them feel welcome to the group. She always has a smile on her face and is usually the first one to tell a joke. What do you think—is she an introvert or an extrovert? Actually, Carmen is an extreme introvert; but her career as a pastor requires her to operate outside of her instinctive style. Because she felt called to the ministry, she took a course in public speaking and human relations to help her get out of her "comfort zone." Now she does those things with seeming effortlessness, but they are still not "comfortable" to her. They are not natural but are learned behaviors.

As you go through this chapter, try to focus on what is "natural" for you—what is instinctive—not what you have learned to do or what is required of you in your family or school or other environment.

Personality Type

Depending on the way you are "wired," you are either considered an introvert or an extrovert. A famous psychiatrist named Carl Jung wrote about the now famous types "introverts" and "extroverts" in 1921. He studied how individuals take in the world, renew their energy, process information, schedule time, and express feelings.

We often use the words *introvert* and *extrovert* incorrectly. You may think of an extrovert as a boisterous, gregarious, outgoing person and of an introvert as being quiet and reserved. Of course, the above description of extrovert may accurately describe some extroverts but not all.

> **Extroverts** are energized through action.
>
> **Introverts** are energized through reflection.

The terms *introvert* or *extrovert* have more to do with the ways in which we use and receive energy than on how verbal we may or may not be. A man named David Keirsey suggests that extroverts gain energy from being with other people, like being powered by batteries. Long periods of quiet and individual work are exhausting for them. Introverts draw energy from solitary activities and working alone. Introverts become exhausted in large groups or from extended contact with others. These examples represent extremes. Most people find themselves somewhere between the two extremes.

Why is it important to understand your personality type when you are considering where to serve? If you're a person who thrives on being with people, and you volunteer to work in a behind-the-scenes role with little opportunity to be with other people, how might that make you feel? Restless? Bored? Closed off? Or if you like to work quietly to accomplish goals with limited interaction with people, how would you feel if you worked in a large group of people with no quiet time to yourself. Don't you think you might be frustrated or uncomfortable?

Even if you think that you know whether your type is more extroverted or introverted, questions in the next section may help you determine your personality type.

What's My Personality Type?

Try to answer, using the word or phrase that best describes what you prefer—not what your home, church, or school life dictates to you. Circle the word or phrase that best matches how you would complete each statement.

I usually *enjoy center stage* or *shun the limelight.*

People who meet me would describe me as *easy to get to know* or *quiet and reserved.*

I develop ideas through *discussion* or *internal thought.*

When my work is interrupted, I *welcome the diversion* or *become impatient with the distraction.*

I work best *in a group* or *independently.*

I prefer to communicate with people by *telephone* or *e-mail.*

When my "batteries" need recharging, I *go out with friends* or *spend some quiet time alone.*

Scoring Your Answers

❖ If you circled the first choice most, you are more likely to be an extrovert.

❖ If you circled the second choice most, you are more likely to be an introvert.

❖ If you're still not sure, consider the following:

—When you're in class, do you tend to "think out loud?"
Or do you usually consider your thoughts and ideas carefully before sharing them?
—When you're tired or stressed out, do you get together with friends to "forget about it"? Or do you need time alone to "chill."
—Do you find it easy to talk to anyone you meet? Or is it easier to talk to people you've known for awhile?

Remember, this is about your instinctive responses, not what you have learned to do.

Most of us fit somewhere in between the two extremes. All day long, we have to move back and forth along the continuum. Take a look at the continuum below and make a mark where you think you fit.

|_____|_____|

Extrovert   Middle   Introvert
(energized   (energized
through   through
interaction)   reflection)

If you find yourself near the middle of the continuum, it may mean that the situation in which you find yourself will dictate your response.

Remember: Extroverts also accomplish tasks and introverts also love people. The purpose of this exercise is to determine which of the two scenarios recharge your batteries and revive your spirit. When you serve God, you will want to be in a place of service where you are energized rather than where you are constantly drained of energy.

Preferred Environment

The term *preferred environment* describes the type of setting in which you prefer to work, play, and function. In order to accomplish the task at hand, people tend to prefer either a stable environment or a flexible one.

People who prefer a stable environment

- like to work with deadlines, structure, accountability
- want to know what to expect and what is expected of them

People who prefer a flexible environment:

- find deadlines, structure, accountability to be confining
- prefer to focus on the end product, leaving the details of how to get there open to change and interpretation

Why is it important to figure out which way you like to do things? If you prefer flexibility in your environment, and you serve in an area that requires you to follow specific steps with little room for "interpretation," how might you feel? Stifled? Bored? Or if you prefer a stable environment and serve in an area where things are always changing, how would you feel? Uncomfortable? Insecure?

You may already know which environment you prefer. In case you don't, the following exercise may help you determine where you might fit on the continuum.

What's My Preferred Environment?

Answer the questions based upon your own preference, not on the situations in which you currently find yourself at home, at school, in your community, or at church.

When I'm working on a project, I like to *adapt as I go* or *plan ahead.*

I tend to work with *spurts of energy* or *regular, steady effort.*

When I plan my activities, the plans are *"penciled in"* or *final.*

I like *spontaneity* or *predictability.*

I tend to *have several projects going on at once* or *finish one thing before going on to the next.*

I prefer decisions that are *open to discussion* or *provide closure.*

I usually dress for *comfort* or *appearance.*

I am more *lighthearted* or *serious.*

Scoring Your Answers

❖ If you circled the first choice most, you are more likely to prefer a flexible environment.

❖ If you circled the second choice most, you are more likely to prefer a stable environment.

❖ If you're still not sure, consider the following:

—Think about a project you have worked on. Did you form a general plan but then adapted and changed course when you thought it appropriate to do so? Or did you plan everything in great detail and follow that plan?
—Do you get more pleasure from starting a project? Or do you get more pleasure from finishing a project?

Look at the continuum below and place a mark where you think you fit on it.

|————————————————————|————————————————————|

Flexible
(adapt
as I go)

Middle

Stable
(plan
ahead)

Putting It All Together

In the space below, write out the combination of energy focus and preferred environment that best describes you (extrovert/stable; extrovert/flexible; introvert/stable; introvert/flexible):

I am _____

(Put this answer on page 56).

Now we'll look at what these style combinations mean when it comes to serving God. Remember, our individuality affects the way we think, receive and expend energy, organize our work, and interact with other people. Let's connect these concepts to serving God in the church and community.

We'll suggest some areas where each of these types might work or serve, but don't be discouraged if the suggestions don't seem right for you. You are unique. Many other considerations to take into account: your spiritual gifts, what you are passionate about, your talents and acquired skills, and so forth.

Extrovert/Stable

❏ If you are an extrovert/stable individual, you are energized by interaction with people.

❏ You will likely prefer to interact with people in predetermined settings and at scheduled times.

❏ You value effectiveness and efficiency, tend to be practical, yet are outgoing and warm.

In the church you may be drawn to people-oriented service opportunities, such as small-group leader, greeter, Sunday school teacher, nursery or preschool worker, usher, intercessory prayer leader.

Some preferred careers for those with this type combination: counselors, social workers, child-care providers, small business owners, healthcare workers, receptionists

A Word of Caution: This type tends to overcommit to work and overinvest emotionally.

Extrovert/Flexible

❏ If you are an extrovert/flexible individual, you are energized by interaction with people.

❏ You enjoy more spontaneity and less structure, more fun and less practicality.

❏ You value creativity, exude enthusiasm, welcome change, and have the capacity to be engaging and inspirational.

In the church, you may be drawn to performing on a drama team, planning new youth group programs, teaching Bible classes, being in a ministry involving team-building, planning events.

Some preferred careers for those with this type combination: politician, actor, marketing personnel, consultant, teacher, sales agent

A Word of Caution: This type may lose sight of important details or have trouble keeping enough focus to accomplish the goal.

Introvert/Stable

❑ If you are an introvert/stable individual, you tend to be quiet, reflective, and practical.

❑ You learn through research and observation.

❑ You value consistency and preservation.

In the church, you may be drawn to edit the youth group newsletter, collate bulletins or mailings, help with audio-visual and computer technology ministries, serve as youth group treasurer.

Some preferred careers for those with this type combination: carpenter, school principal, clergy person, military officer, accountant

A Word of Caution: This type can exhibit nit-picking tendencies, can become bogged down with details or lose sight of the "big picture."

Introvert/Flexible

❑ If you are an introvert/flexible individual, you tend to be direct, visionary, focused, confident, and competitive.

❑ You enjoy meeting challenges and making decisions.

❑ You value results, big dreams, thorough research, and independent thinking.

In the church, you may be drawn to leading a mission trip, teaching Sunday school, leading youth group discussions, organizing a campaign or event.

Some preferred careers for those with this type combination: lawyer, architect, manager or executive, engineer, journalist, physician

A Word of Caution: This type may be perceived as pushy, controlling, or arrogant and would do well to remember that the thoughts, ideas, and contributions of others are valuable and necessary.

Conclusion

Every aspect of church and community life would benefit from having each of the four combinations represented. A ministry or program stands a better chance of succeeding with each of these in balance. Strong youth groups will include a variety of personalities and preferred environment types, with everyone contributing his or her own uniqueness to the mix.

People won't always fit neatly on a grid or continuum. Human beings are much more complex and diverse; that makes life more interesting! Yet knowing our individual style—and the style of those with whom we interact—can provide important clues to help us communicate more effectively, avoid conflict, articulate our needs, and serve with less frustration and more joy. That's what God wants for us—a place to serve and glorify God where we can be our best selves, fulfilling God's perfect design.

Chapter 6: Dreams and Experience

Hope deferred makes the heart sick,
  but a desire fulfilled is a tree of life.
                                    (Proverbs 13:12)

The "D" and "E" in our S.T.R.I.D.E. help us remember to pay attention to our *dreams* and *experience* as we seek to use our gifts. God cares about every need that exists on earth. God does not want anyone be hurt, sick, alone, or lost. God counts on us to be God's hands and voice in this broken world; but God knows that we, as individuals, can't possibly care about every need. For that reason, much like a parent dividing household chores among children, God places a dream (a desire, a passion, a calling) in each of our hearts.

Unlike household chores, though, the dream is accompanied by passion for the calling. Because we are passionate about it, we are happy and effective when we are serving in that area. If each of us understands the dream that God has given us, and fulfills that calling, the Body of Christ can meet every need, heal every hurt, and save every lost lamb. Isn't it exciting to think that if every Christian found his or her passion, and served in that area, the world could be drastically changed as God worked through each of us?

Where would you like to make a difference? Some people are clear about their calling. One person may be passionate about getting other students at their high school to consistently recycle. Another is passionate about making sure homeless people have warm shelter in the winter months. Someone else seeks to make everyone aware about the crisis in Darfur.

What if you haven't yet figured out what God may be calling you to do? How do you discover your dreams? Os Guinness, author of *The Call: Finding and Fulfilling the Central Purpose of Your Life*, writes, "In many cases, a clear sense of calling comes only through a time of searching, including trial and error." If you have never been exposed to the area in which God wants you to serve, you probably will not recognize it until you do try it out.

Finding a calling through trial and error can be intimidating. It means taking risks and just trying something. Such risks are worthwhile because they make us dependent on God, not on ourselves. When we try to serve in a new area, we blaze a trail in our life. Having the faith to risk stepping out of our comfort zone stretches us and makes the journey more real.

In many cases, a youth group and church offer an environment where you can take such a risk. You're young; you're supposed to try new things. And with a group of supporters, you can be free to take risks—even to fail. If you do, your friends will pick you up, brush you off, and put you back on the road again. Maybe they'll even help you find a different saddle.

Like most people, you might sometimes be afraid to be called into an area that seems beyond your capabilities or experience. For example, what if you've never prayed in front of the entire congregation? Or although you want to try a Habitat for Humanity work day, you can hardly hammer a nail straight? Thankfully, it's not your own capabilities or experience on which you have to rely but on the power of the Holy Spirit.

In his book *What You Do Best in the Body of Christ*, Bruce Bugbee lists three types of dreams that seem to pop up again and again for individuals or groups of people:

1. dreams of making a difference for individual persons or groups of people;
2. dreams of making a difference in connection with some worthwhile cause;
3. dreams of making a difference through some role or function.

For example, some persons may dream of helping specific groups of people, such as elderly people in a nursing home, or abused children. Others may dream of conquering AIDS, or hunger, or homelessness. Still others may dream of making a difference as a mentor in Big Brothers/Big Sisters or by using specific skills or gifts. Don't limit your dreams to these categories, though; your dreams may fall outside them.

Discovering your dream and then actually fulfilling it can change your life. Serving in an area about which you are passionate is a blessing. It provides a compass to give you direction about where to serve, motivation and energy to help you avoid burnout, joy and fulfillment to reflect your dreams that are becoming reality.

> But those who wait for the LORD shall renew their strength,
>   they shall mount up with wings like eagles,
>   they shall run and not be weary,
>   they shall walk and not faint.
>
> (Isaiah 40:31)

Finding Your Dreams 1

Take time to answer the following questions that may point you in the direction of your dreams:

❍ What excites you most about the world?

❍ What angers you most about the world?

❍ What would you do if you had time and money to do anything?

❍ What do you enjoy doing so much that time seems to fly when you're doing it?

❍ What do your friends and family think you are passionate about?

❍ For what are you most grateful today? For what are you least grateful? If you were to ask yourself these questions every day, what pattern would you see?

❍ When have you felt most alive? What are the times of your life you would most like to repeat?

❍ If you could do anything with no chance of failure, what would you do?

❍ Is there something that you have to do that you can't not do? If so, what?

❍ If you only had one year to live, what would you do?

Look for patterns in your answers. Are there issues or topics that keep coming up? Ask those who know you what they think your passions might be. Try using the process of elimination to discover where you dream. (For starters, you might think about what you don't want to do.) For instance, a youth named Brian admits, "I don't get all excited about the big issues like hunger or homelessness or famine in an African country. I care in a general way, but it feels very distant. I'm not comfortable with small children. I don't feel comfortable in front of large groups. I love to work with my hands, and I've figured out a lot of electrical wiring on my own by reading books. So when I heard about Sierra Service Project, where I could help Native Americans renovate their homes on reservations, I was really excited."

Finding Your Dreams 2

❍ What particular age group of people do you enjoy being with? Are there age groups with whom you would prefer not to work?

❍ With what groups of people do you feel drawn to work (homeless, abused children, incarcerated youth)? With which specific groups do I not want to work?

❍ What activities (such as gardening, music, sports) do you really enjoy that you would like to incorporate into ministry?

❍ Look over your three spiritual gifts (on page 56). Is there one that you would enjoy using regardless of the situation?

❍ Look at your list of natural talents and (on page 56). Which of these would you like to put to use, even if you don't have a specific area of service in mind?

❍ Is there a need that you have noticed and feel drawn to seeing addressed?

❍ Have you been involved in service in the past that you really enjoyed and in which you would like to be involved again? Is there something else you have tried in which you did not feel fulfilled and/or effective? What made these experiences positive or negative for you?

❍ Finding your dream is a journey not an event. It often requires trying a few things to see whether you like them. This should be a prayerful process. Ask for God's guidance, and be patient; this might take a while. Once you discover your dreams, you cannot help but work to see them realized. They are like an emotional magnet drawing you in.

If I say, "I will not mention him, or speak any more in his name," then within me there is something like a burning fire shut up in my bones; I am weary with holding it in, and I cannot. (Jeremiah 20:9)

Finding My Dreams 3

Based on what I know now, my dream is
(Write this on page 56.)

Don't get discouraged if you're not yet sure what your dream is. You've got plenty of time. You may try different areas of service to see what draws you in. Ask your youth leader or pastor to discuss possibilities for service with you. Even if you just start with a general idea of what you want to do, over time your focus can narrow and become clearer.

Trust God to reveal your dream in God's own time.

Experiences

We know that all things work together for good for those who love God, who are called according to his purpose. (Romans 8:28)

Whether you're fourteen, fifteen, sixteen, seventeen, or eighteen, you have a past. Good or bad, our experiences make us who we are today. Some people give themselves credit for the good things that happen to them and blame God for the bad. The reality is that we aren't responsible for all the good experiences, and God doesn't cause the bad experiences to happen to us—but God does use our experiences to fulfill God's purposes.

For example, Ryan's family moved almost every year. He had attended nine schools by the time he was a junior in high school. Although Ryan sometimes wished that he'd been able to grow up in one neighborhood, keep his childhood friends all the way through high school, and enjoy that continuity, he also realized that all of the moving had made him very resilient. "I can make friends anywhere, anytime," he says. "I became extremely adaptable to new situations." Ryan was able to find the gift of his experience.

Alicia's parents divorced amicably when she was four. She quickly got into the every-other-weekend routine and learned to feel comfortable at both parents' homes. "As torn up about the divorce as I was when I was little, I ended up with two separate families, both great, who love me and have given me different things," she says now. "I love my little half-brother to pieces, and have learned how to function in two different family structures. Sure, I would've preferred that my parents stay together; but in some ways, I'm stronger because they didn't. I'm probably more independent than if I had stayed with one set of parents."

Learn From Experience

What have been some of the formative experiences in your life? You may not remember every situation yourself for those early years, but you may have heard stories from your parents or other adults. For each of the time periods below, write the most significant accomplishments or important experiences, both positive and negative:

Preschool

Grades K–3

Grades 4–6

Middle School

High School

Strengths and traits from these experiences: (Place sticky notes here.)
(Write some of these on page 56.)

This Is Who I Am

Spiritual Gifts—my three highest-scoring gifts (in order) are (from page 19):

1.

2.

3.

Talents (from page 39):

Resources (from page 40):

Individuality—I believe that my style is (from page 47):

Dreams—I sense I have a passion for (from page 54):

Experiences—Strengths and traits I have because of my experiences are (from page 55):

Possible areas of service, ministry, and/or involvement in my church and community:

I am already involved in the ministry area of: